WEATHERING THE GLOBAL CRISIS: CAN THE TRAITS OF ISLAMIC BANKING SYSTEM MAKE A DIFFERENCE?

SITI ZALEHA ABDUL RASID
MOHAMAD AZHAR NIZAM
WAN KHAIRUZZAMAN WAN ISMAIL

PARTRIDGE
A Penguin Random House Company

To order additional copies of this book, contact
Toll Free 800 101 2657 (Singapore)
Toll Free 1 800 81 7340 (Malaysia)
orders.singapore@partridgepublishing.com

www.partridgepublishing.com/singapore

CONTENTS

Islamic Banking and Globalisation

Overview

Globalisation has led to a systemic threat to the financial crisis that can cause chaos to financial systems and economies across the globe. The 2008 global financial crisis which started with the sub-prime mortgage has unveiled series of unscrupulous risk taking activities by financial institutions in the United States. Excessive risk taking, creative camouflaging of risks, creation of artificial demand through securitisation and speculative activities have been fuelling the ballooning real estate prices in the US since the 1990s which ran out of steam in 2007; posing systematic risk of widespread failures throughout the financial system in the US as well as other dependent economies such as Europe. Amongst the casualties of the 2008 global financial crisis includes big financial institutions such as AIG, Lehman Brothers and Northern Rock Building Society in the UK.

Since the 1980s, Regulators of the financial markets namely the Bank of International Settlements (BIS) based in Basel, Switzerland have been worried about the exponential growth of globalised banking and the interconnectivity of economies on global scale whilst at the same time, capital ratios of main international banks did not increase at the same pace. Subsequent to the 1974 collapse of Herstatt Bank in West Germany, The Basel Committee on

Banking Supervision (the Basel Committee) was established as a forum for cooperation amongst its member countries on banking supervisory matters and the Basel Committee has issued a capital adequacy framework to ensure banks are well capitalised to weather any losses suffered due to the effects of globalisation. This capital adequacy framework often referred to as the Basel Accord has the objective to provide a common capital measurement system and acts as regulatory tool to ensure banks do not take excessive risk without having the minimum required capital to undertake such risks (*History of the Basel Committee and its Membership,* Bank of International Settlement, 2009).

The first Basel Accord was issued in 1988 and later revised in June 1999 and in 2010 in the wake of the 2008 global financial crisis. Under the 1988 Basel I Accord, banks are required to have a minimum Risk Weighted Capital Adequacy Ratio (RWCAR) of 8%. The RWCAR is important as it shows the level of healthiness of Banks across the globe. The Basel Accord is meant to be a regulatory tool as well as a mechanism for discipline and transparency reporting for banks. This is supported by the findings made by Mendoca, Galvao and Loure (2011) in their research on how the Brazilian banks are able to weather the subprime crisis in 2008.

Islamic banking is a form of banking based on the rules and regulation of Islamic Shariah laws which prohibited interest/usury or riba' as it does not perceived money to have an intrinsic value but instead, Islamic finance or Islamic banking is based on asset (Alexakis and Tsikouras, 2009). In Malaysia, Islamic banking started with the establishment of Bank Islam Malaysia Berhad on July 1983 under the Islamic Banking Act 1983. The second Islamic Bank in Malaysia is Bank Muamalat Malaysia Berhad, established in 1993. Due to the liberation made by the Central Bank of Malaysia (Bank Negara Malaysia or BNM), since 2006, there has been a mushrooming of Islamic Banks in the Malaysian financial market with some are direct subsidiaries of foreign banks such as

Kuwait Finance House, Al Rajhi Bank and Asian Finance Bank Berhad. Currently, there are sixteen (16) Islamic Banks operating in Malaysia (refer to Appendix 1).

Chazi & Syed (2010) and Ahmed (2010) have argued that Islamic banks globally were able to weather the adverse effects from the financial crisis in 2008 due to the risk aversion mechanisms inherent in basic Islamic finance principles such as prohibition of riba' and gambling, concept of social justice and No Reward without Risk (*al ghonm-bil ghorm*). Similar to other form of business whereby there is separation between ownership and management, banks are run by professional managers and based on agency theory, also subject to the information asymmetry.

Shareholders aim to maximise shareholders wealth whilst the management's main objective is to increase revenue and returns in the form of wages and bonuses. This might be at the expense of overall profitability which is more important to the shareholders.

Therefore, Corporate Governance also plays a significant role in the running of banks (both internal and externally) in Malaysia. Banks in Malaysia is subjected to the rulings and regulations issued by the Bank Negara Malaysia and/or the Securities Commission. In addition to that Islamic banks in particular, given that Islamic Finance is derived from the Shariah laws, Islamic banks are also subjected to internal governance structure in the form of Shariah Advisory/Supervisory Board (SSB) and to the external governance issued by the several governance standards or directives issued by external regulatory bodies such as The Accounting and Auditing Organisation for Islamic Financial Institutions (AAOIFI), the Islamic Financial Services Board (IFSB), the Shariah Committee of central banks and regulators (e.g. the Shariah Advisory Panels of Bank Negara Malaysia and Securities Commission).

Past studies conducted have shown that firms performance have subjected to the strength of its Corporate Governance and some due to the characteristics of the firm or its industry. Common corporate governance and firm characteristics variables noted based on past studies include but not limited to the size of the Board of Directors (BOD), the composition of the BOD, CEO duality, industry type, organisational complexity, the reputation of auditors, firm size and concentration of ownership.

In light of the study conducted by Chazi & Syed (2010) and Ahmed (2010) on the ability of Islamic banks in weathering the 2008 global financial crisis, this study attempts to assess whether there is relationship between the corporate governance and firm characteristics variables in the RWCAR recorded by Islamic banks in Malaysia post 2008 global financial crisis.

Therefore, this book tries to quantify the strength of the relationships between corporate governance and firm characteristics (which are both considered western based concepts) by looking the risks ratios obtained from the financial statements of the Islamic Banks in Malaysia for up to four (3) consecutive years after the beginning of the financial crisis (FYE2008, FYE2009 and FYE2011). Due to the differentials in financial year end for some Islamic Banks in Malaysia, some of the Islamic Banks in the study has already published their FYE2012 and if it is made available, the data is also included in the study.

The September 11, 2001 incident has proliferated the Islamophobia in the United States to stratospheric levels and inadvertently, partly responsible for the shift of capital from the West to the other parts of the world by oil rich Middle East business people who are now being marginalised by the West due to their religious beliefs. This has in some ways, (in addition to the religious conscience in obtaining 'halal' or permissible investments) helped fuelled the growth of Islamic Finance in non-traditional markets such Malaysia and the United Arab Emirates (UAE).

The financial crisis in 2008 saw excessive risk taking, creative camouflaging of risks, creation of artificial demand through securitisation and speculative activities. All these led to swelling estate prices in the US since the 1990s, posing systematic risk of widespread failures throughout the global financial system.

However, it is during these trying periods, Islamic banks were shielded from the adverse effects of the financial meltdown in the West and this mainly due to the fact that their operations are based on the principles of Islamic finances that not only prohibits interest (riba') based transactions but also prohibits transactions with excessive uncertainty (Gharar) which resulted in substantial losses to conventional banks, particularly in the Western world (Chazi & Syed, 2010).

As such, taking cue from the works done by several scholars, the authors attempt to establish the relationship in the investment behaviour exemplified by risk aversion of the Malaysian Islamic bank and their risk based financial performance measured by the capital adequacy ratios as outlined by the Basel Committee. Given that investment behaviour is a by-product of the Management's conscious decision making, which in theory is guided by the Corporate Governance and risk management structures embedded in the Islamic banks themselves, it is interesting to see how far is Corporate Governance (GC) and Firm Characteristics (FC) have contributed to this.

Why the Study?

In 2012, the global economy is bogged down with the lethargic economic recovery in the United States which only grew by 2.1% y-o-y and its manufacturing sector has not fully recovered with its Purchasing Managers Index (PMI) is at its lowest for the past 3 years, consequent of the 2008 global financial crisis. To add salt to the wound, the Eurozone economy for the main part of 2012 is also doubtful as member-countries such as Greece and Spain are on the verge of defaulting on their sovereign loans. Therefore, in order to bring those ailing economies back on the rebound, the global economy must be convinced that banking systems are still intact and in order to do that, the Risk Weighted Capital Adequacy Ratio (RWCAR) of the banks in the US and the Eurozone must improve or at least, seen to be improving.

However, those banks, in the first place, have conformed to the standard set by the Basel Committee of the Bank of International Settlement (BIS). As pointed out by Chazi & Syed (2010), Adel Ahmed (2010) and Tahir & Brimble (2011) earlier, most if not all Islamic Banks are weathered from the recent 2008 global financial crisis even though they inherit and conform to the same Corporate Governance (CG) structure and capital adequacy framework imposed by the Basel Committee.

The authors seeks whether relationship exist between corporate governance variables such as board size, CEO duality or firm characteristics such as size or percentage of foreign ownership with the level of risk based performance exemplified by Risk Weighted Capital Adequacy Ratio (RWCAR) of Islamic Banks in Malaysia post 2008 global financial crisis. The findings will be useful to the industry because they illustrate why Islamic banks specifically in Malaysia are able to weather the aftermath of the 2008 global financial crisis which at the point of writing, still affect some parts of the world including the United States and the Eurozone with sovereign debt defaults, which are unheard off before.

Islamic Finance and Islamic Banking in Malaysia

Islam in its simplest literary definition means peace and obedience. In its simplest contextual meaning refers to 'total submission to one God (i.e. Allah S.W.T) by doing what is permissible and leaving the activities that is prohibited by God'.

Based on Hussain (2004), Islam derives the laws (Shariah) from two (2) main sources namely the primary sources of the Quran and the Sunnah (the words and actions of the Prophet Muhammad PBUH) and the secondary sources of Ijtihad (the interpretations/ opinions of learned jurists). Ijitihad is achieved via two means:

i) Ijma, the consensus of opinion of Islamic scholars based on Quran and Sunnah; and

ii) Qiyas, which is simply reasoning by analogy.

In any case, the primary sources would take precedent over the secondary sources.

Sources of Islamic Finance

Islamic Finance derived its permissibility from the Holy Decree by Allah S.W.T. in the Quranic verse as follows:

"Those who devour riba will not stand except as stands one from the evil one by his touch has been driven to madness. That is because they say: Trade is like riba. But Allah hath permitted trade and forbidden riba. Those who, after receiving directions from their Lord, desist shall be pardoned, for the past their case is for Allah to judge. But those who repeat (the offence) are companions of the fire. They will abide therein forever." (Surah Al Baqarah, Verse: 275, Chapter 2, Quran)

Under the decree, Allah S.W.T. has also provided one of the main tenets of Islamic Finance which is the prohibition of riba' (usury). Nevertheless, Allah S.W.T. has provided the alternative to riba' which is trade and this forms the basis of Islamic finance: Islamic banks are also trading houses, which assumes the risk of partnerships and the risk involves in trading via *shariah* compliant/ *shariah* based mode of financing.

Due the permissibility of trading, Islamic banks provide financial services to their customers based several main categories of contracts:

i) Profit and Loss sharing (PLS) contracts such as *Musyarakah* (Joint Venture) and *Mudharabah* (Partnership);

ii) Sales based contracts such as *Murabahah* (cost plus), *Istisna'* (contract financing), *Ijarah* (leasing), *Bai As-Salam* (forward contract); and

iii) Fee based contracts such as *Ujrah* (fees), *Wadiah* (safekeeping), *Wakalah* (agency) and *Rahnu* (pawnbroking).

The development of Islamic Banking in Malaysia

It can be argued that the adoption of Islamic finance in Malaysia started with the establishment of the Perbadanan Wang Simpanan Bakal-Bakal Haji or Tabung Haji or The Pilgrims Fund in September 1963 to assist the Muslims in Malaysia in financing their pilgrimage to Mecca.

However, the full-fledged Islamic Banking in Malaysia started with the establishment of Bank Islam Malaysia Berhad on 1 July 1983 under the Islamic Banking Act 1983. Bank Islam Malaysia Berhad (BIMB) was later listed on the Bursa Malaysia Berhad (formerly known as Kuala Lumpur Stock Exchange or KLSE). The second full-fledged Islamic bank, Bank Muamalat Malaysia Berhad was established some 10 years later in 1993.

Since the 1990s, most commercial banks in Malaysia has been serving their customers that opted for Islamic banking products through their *Skim Perbankan Tanpa Faedah* (SPTF) or Non-Interest Bearing Banking Scheme windows but later transformed their Islamic Banking portfolio into a separate Islamic Banking subsidiary to cater to the growing market.

Main Tenets of Islamic Finance

The cornerstone of Islamic Finance is derived from the Quranic revelation under Verse 275 of Surah Al Baqarah that the God has permitted trading as means to wealth and at the same time prohibit riba'. That single verse alone has suggested two main key concepts of which Islamic finance and Muamalat (interactions and relationship between humans with specific emphasis on economic activities) are based upon, namely:

i) Wealth is encouraged in Islamic and God has provided that trading as a means to gaining such wealth in a truthful and honest way;

ii) In the pursuit for wealth, God has prohibited usury. Usury in this context does not only confine to the charge of interest or unperturbed growth in value (without commensurations of work, risk taking and responsibility). It is worth to note that the concept of riba' under this Verse also extends to any form of injustice;

iii) The concept of trading mentioned in the Verse is twofold as it involves counterparties (e.g. suppliers and/or clients). This verse also compels for Muslim to seek bounty and wealth through cementing cooperation with other Muslims (hence, the word Trading) and foster good relationship.

Therefore, suffice to say that based on that single verse alone, God has provided that wealth and bounty is to be pursued by rightful ways so long as the means do not inflict any form of injustice.

Prohibition of Usury (Riba') and The Permissibility of Trade

Based on the Verse 275, Surah Al Baqarah, Allah S.W.T has strictly prohibited usury (riba') and provided the alternative in the form of trading.

However, it needs to be pointed out that trading of non-permissible items and activities such as pork, non-Islamic slaughter of livestocks, liquor and its derivatives and activities that contain elements of gambling (maysir) or uncertainty (gharar) are still prohibited as pointed by the Verse 55, Surah Ar Rahman of the Al Quran as follows:

"Avoiding unlawful things in selling"

(Verse 55, Surah Ar Rahman, Chapter 9, Al Quran).

Prophet Muhammad PBUH has listed such *ribawi* items as follows:

   i)   Gold
   ii) Silver
   iii) Dates
   iv) Barley
   v) Wheat; and
   vi) Salt

Based on the hadith or written narration recorded by Al Bukhari, Prophet Muhammad PBUH has mentioned that if these ribawi items were to be traded, it must be traded equally: size, weight, quality, value and must be exchanged at the same time to avoid riba'(Hadith Al Bukhari, Volume 3, Book 34, Number 382).

Some scholars have extended this rule to include other food materials whilst some scholars only restricted to the items that have been historically used as a medium of exchange to facilitate trade.

Islam recognises money as a medium of exchange and not as a commodity that can be traded. Unlike commodities that can be transformed into a useful end product, money on its own does not have any other useful functions (although gold can be melted into jewellery, without the smelting process, gold on its own does not have a useful function). Therefore, the exchange of money between parties does not involve the element of work or risk; from which the profits derived cannot be of positive economic consequences to the other party.

Riba' in Islamic is not directly related to interest which is the price of borrowed money but instead relates to the growth in money or other ribawi items without the corresponding or commensurating increase in the capital wealth stock in the economic system. There should not be any reward for passivity in Islam. This main reason behind the prohibition of riba' is to ensure that economic growth in a certain economy is based on real demand and no artificial demand created by the illusion caused by money is able to multiply itself through riba' activities and consequently, providing the holders of capital unjustified advantage over others (Chopra, 1992 and Al-Awan (2006)).

The Concept of Economic and Social Justice

One of the cornerstones of Islamic Economics is founded on the premises of Brotherhood and Economic and Social Justice. Social justice extends under the umbrella of muamalah (human relations with each other). This means that Islamic Finance intends to achieve the following:

i) To foster cooperation amongst economic units (government, household and firms) to safeguard faith, life, intellect, posterity and property (Imam Al Ghazali, 11th Century);

ii) To achieve a balanced and sustainable widespread economic growth (Al-Awan (2006));

iii) Encourages moderation and prohibits excesses including behaviour towards risk in wealth generation (Rosly and Zaini, 2008).

Therefore, Islamic economics (thus, Islamic Finance) activities must exclude any elements of uncertainty (gharar), gambling (maysir), oppression (such as monopoly or any forms of favouritism) and unproductive or excessive risk taking activities (such as hedonism, illegal racing, production of harmful chemicals etc) and must aim to achieve the greater good of humanity as a whole.

Under this tenet also is the reason why interest is prohibited by Islam. Interest is a predetermined rate of return of a financing activity that burdens the borrower and at the same time, guarantees the return for the lender.

No Reward Without Risk

Many Islamic scholars based on the sources from the Hadith and Al Quran has already established that for profit from a trade to be lawful, it must consist of the following elements:

i) *Kasb* or effort. For a certain trade to be lawful, the element of work or effort in the transaction must be present and not one party transaction. For example, for trading of chicken would require the seller to acquire the chicken before selling them to the buyers in the market. Islam allows this effort to be rewarded in the form of profit.

ii) *Ghomn* or risk taking. The same chicken trader has assumed the risk of the chicken unable to be delivered to the market during transportation. Islam has allowed this profit as the chicken trade has assumed the risk in his/her pursuit of profit.

iii) Daman or responsibility for the sale. A chicken trader would normally be held liable if the chicken being sold is not Halal for example. If the chicken trader does not assume the responsibility for his/her stock of chickens to the customers, the profit under that transaction is considered unlawful or haram. This is based on the hadith of the Prophet (pbuh): "You will be responsible for what you have done".

In the context of Islamic Banks, all the products offered by the Bank should, in theory conforms to all three (3) elements.

The Concept of Separate Legal Entity and

Agency Theory

Under the law, a company incorporated as a limited liability company is considered a separate legal entity from the shareholders of the company. The company on its own is a legal person which, similar to a normal person, is able to assume liabilities, to sue or be sued, enter contracts and own property.

The principle of separate legal entity is premised on the judgment of the common law case of Salomon vs. Salomon (1897) and the case thereafter, has been the cornerstone of Company Law worldwide. The Salomon vs. Salomon case have set the precedent that the company is a separate legal entity which is distinct from its shareholders which are only liable to extent of the capital which they have contributed.

However, given that the company is not a physical being, policy and procedures and governance structure are constructed. The role of overseeing and setting the policies and structures of the company rests on the Board of Directors, which are the representatives of the shareholders duly appointed during the General Meetings. The Board of Directors derived their powers from the delegation of power made by the shareholders and has the objective to act on the best interest of the shareholders (Section 126, Malaysia Companies Act 1965).

In addition to that, to ensure the smooth running of the daily operations of the company, the Board of Director shall subsequently delegate part of the powers vested to them onto a team of managers and set the strategies and targets for these managers. These managers are employees of the company and have their own different objectives; which often conflict with the objectives of the Board of Directors and/or the shareholders (Kim, 2011).

Introduction to Corporate Governance

There have been various studies on Corporate Governance but there has not been a universal definition of Corporate Governance. In simple terms, Corporate Governance relates to the system of which companies or corporations are being managed and controlled.

Mustapha and Che Ahmad (2011) have defined Corporate Governance as the process and guidelines that are being used to manage and direct the business activities of a company to increase its shareholders' wealth.

From an Islamic finance perspective, Al-Awan from INCEIF had in 2006 defined Corporate Governance to be the moral and ethical dimensions of managing business and man as a moral being, is at the centre of its operations (taken from An Overview of Islamic and Conventional Economics & Financial Theories, Chartered Islamic Finance Professional (CIFP), pp 1-24, INCEIF).

Corporate Governance is the set of systems, principles and processes by which a company is governed (Thomson, 2009). It relates to the mechanisms, regulations and relationships between the shareholders of the company, their appointed management teams and other stakeholders such as suppliers, creditors, governments and so on.

As implied in the previous section, there have been several layers of delegation of powers from the shareholders to the managers of the company. With the dilution of power, the shareholders also have diluted their control over the company as the managers and shareholders have different objectives.

Introduction to Firms Characteristics

A firm's characteristic are the ways the firms is able to be identified and distinguished from the other firms. This can come in various ways that a firm can be identified.

Amongst the common firm characteristics that is often used include:

i) Type of Industry that it is operating;
ii) Ownership/shareholding structure; which refers to level of ownership by different groups of shareholders or the level of ownership concentration. Types of shareholding structure varies from an organisation that is controlled by a family, government controlled via Government Linked Companies or in the extreme cases, there are conglomerates with layers and myriad of complex shareholdings structure whereby the suppliers and customers are shareholders of each other. A typical example of these complex shareholding structures are the Keiretsus of Japan or Chaebols of Korea (Kim, 2011);

iii) Firm Size. There are also many measures for firm size. For example, revenue, shareholders funds, total assets or number of employees are often used to categorise whether a company is considered Large, Medium or Small.

Small and Medium Enterprise Corporation Malaysia (SMECorp) has defined Small Medium Enterprises (SME) as follows:

Table 1: SME Corporation Malaysia's Categorisation of Firm Size

Type of Industry	Micro Enterprise	Small Enterprise	Medium Enterprise	Large Enterprise
Manufacturing, Manufacturing Related Services and Agro based industries	• Sales turnover of less than RM250,000; or • Full time employee less than 5	• Sales turnover between RM250,000 and less than RM10 million; or • Full time employee between 5 and 50	• Sales turnover between RM10.0 million and RM25 million; or • Full time employee between 51 and 150	• Sales turnover more than RM25 million; or • Full time employee more than 150
Services, Primary Agriculture and Information & Communication Technology (ICT)	• Sales turnover of less than RM200,000; or • Full time employees less than 5.	• Sales turnover between RM200,000 and less than RM1 million; or • Full time employee between 5 and 19	• Sales turnover between RM1.0 million and RM5 million; or • Full time employee between 20 and 50	• Sales turnover more than RM5 million; or • Full time employee more than 50

Source: SME Corp Malaysia (http://www.smecorp.gov.my/v4/node/14)

Corporate Governance, Capital Adequacy and Risk Capital

At the turn of the new millennium, consequent to the demise of Enron and the following corporate scandal in large firms such as WorldCom, the issue of Corporate Governance has been put into the limelight once again. When talking about Corporate Governance, one cannot avoid but to start with the classic issue of Agency Theory and that is where this section of the literature review shall commence its journey.

Given the scope of the study, the section shall also venture briefly into the history of corporate governance and shall slowly focus on the Malaysian context of Islamic banking.

Agency Theory—Separation between Ownership and Management

The principal-agent problem, agency dilemma or agency theory exist in the situation whereby the owners of a certain organisation (shareholders or stakeholders) are separated from the running of the organisation (the management). This situation is prevalent in the corporate world whereby the business is incorporated and thus, from the legal point of view, created a separate legal entity. The organisation itself has become distinct from its shareholders and although it is a separate legal entity on itself, the running of its activities requires the appointment of agents or managers to increase the efficiency by engaging the expertise of professional managers (Kim, 2011).

Subramaniam, McManus and Zhang (2009) has outlined that an agency relationship occurs under contract whereby one party engages another as an agent to perform certain task/service on their behalf. The shareholders enter into a contract with the management to administer the organisation or business on their behalf and generally assumed to be acting on the best interest of the shareholders (Jensen and Meckling, 1976; Lambert, 2001). However, the two parties have differing interests, motivations and perceptions. Shareholders aim to maximise their wealth whilst the management's main objective is to increase revenue and returns in the form of wages, bonus etc. which may compromise overall profitability.

Given that the delegation of powers of running the business has been granted to the management, every decision made during the daily operations of the organisation lies with the management and would only be made known at a very much later stage to the shareholders during the annual general meeting. By then, any damages made would have been too late and the shareholders are in the worse off position.

Alnasser (2012) has opined that the corporate governance does not merely involve the relationship between shareholders and managers but also extends the scope involving other stakeholders such as creditors and governments. Given so, these stakeholders are often much worse off than shareholders as they do not have the immediate power of rectification or even the power of first information as the appointment of the Board of Directors or even the Management Team is not theirs to yield. These stakeholders would have to depend on signalling from the market or intelligence provided by external parties such as rating agencies, credit investigators and the sort.

The Case for Corporate Governance

The Securities Commission of Malaysia (SC), the regulator for the capital markets in Malaysia has defined Corporate Governance as follows:

"The process and structure used to direct and manage the business and affairs of the company towards enhancing business prosperity and corporate accountability with the ultimate objective of realising long term shareholder value, whilst taking into account of the interests of other stakeholders" (Malaysian Code on Corporate Governance, 2012).

Embong, Mohd Salleh and Hassan (2012) has argued that information asymmetry exist when certain parties have more information than others in a given transaction; therefore, enabling those with more information to take advantage of the other parties with less information. This would indefinitely result in two main problems of adverse selection and moral hazard.

Due to information asymmetry, certain governance mechanisms are incorporated into the administration of the organisation. This is dealt using internal and external mechanisms. The most common mechanisms used are the appointment of Board of Directors as an internal monitoring mechanism and the use of external auditors as the external mechanism (Adams, 1994; Baiman, 1990; Jensen and Meckling, 1976; Lamber, 2001; Subramaniam, 2006).

Based on Subramaniam, McManus and Zhang (2009), the shareholders have two major avenues in mitigating the costs of monitoring the management via:

i)   Installing auditing and other governance mechanisms that aligns the behaviour of the agents with the interests of the shareholders; and

ii) Provide performance based reward structure that incentivised the agent to act in the best interests of the shareholders.

However, these mechanisms however do not come free and often costly and the cost of monitoring is often referred to Agency Costs and Agency Cost comes in the form of monitoring costs, bonding costs and residual costs. These costs are able to be reduced by establishing Corporate Governance mechanisms by enhancing the role of the Board of Directors (Kim, 2011).

Realising the need to tame the differentiating conflict of interest posed by the management against the interests of the stakeholders, evidenced by the scams and failures in the corporate sectors in the UK in the 1980s, the Financial Reporting Council, the London Stock Exchange and the accounting fraternity had in May 1991 (with the blessing of the ruling Conservative Party) established the 'Cadbury Committee'.

The Cadbury Committee which was headed by Sir Adrian Cadbury had the ultimate aim to address the problems relating to agency costs and the ways that these agency costs can be meaningfully addressed through corporate governance and to provide recommendations for the BOD to implement such corporate governance.

The Cadbury Committee had released their first inaugural guidelines and recommendation in the Report and Code of Best Practise in December 1992. The report was subsequently, across the globe referred to as the "Cadbury Report".

Amongst the salient recommendations made by the Cadbury Report (made concise) are:

i) Frequency of Board meeting. By having the Board meeting on more frequent basis, the Board of Directors would be to retain full and effective control over the Management and the decisions made in their absence and provide remedies or solutions on a more timely basis;

ii) The role on Non-Executive Directors. The Cadbury Report provided recommendation that the greater number of non executive directors is needed to balance the power and influence of the executive directors during the BOD meeting.

By having a more balanced Board would ensure a better check and balance on the decisions, policies and directives made by the Board that will indefinitely affect the direction of the organisation and ways it conducts its operations;

iii) Financial reporting and internal controls.

The Cadbury Report has been adopted by various organisations as reference in developing their own internal governance structures. The recommendations made by the Cadbury Report have been used by the likes of the World Bank, the United States and the European Union.

Corporate Governance via Board Committees

Even by having the power to elect the member of the Board of Directors (BOD) might not be enough to reduce the gap to ensure enhancing shareholders value is the main agenda for managers. This is because due to the availability of the Board members, Board meetings are not frequent and only fed outdated information. In response to that, the subcommittees accountable to the Board of Directors are established in firms across the globe. Subramaniam, McManus and Zhang (2009) has posited that formation of BOD sub committees is associated systematically with organisational and corporate governance factors.

Furthermore, due to the globalisation and ever increasing complexity of doing business in a more globalised world whereby decisions and communication needed to be prompt and precise, a more proactive role of the Board of Directors are required. In response to the foregoing, the Board of Directors subsequently delegate part of its approving and supervisory powers to the sub-committees.

Brick and Chidambaran (2010) had also agreed to the foregoing when they placed intensity of BOD activity as an important dimension of BOD oversight on the running of an organisation.

Mostly, these sub-committees are led by at least one (1) member of the Board of Directors. Examples of the commonly used sub-committees are Nomination Committees (NC), Audit Committee (AC), Remuneration Committees (RC) and Risk Management Committee (RMC). Due to the smaller size of the BOD sub committees, the meetings are able to be made more frequent and the scope of such subcommittees is more focussed.

Various studies have been conducted on BOD sub-committees such as Chau and Leung (2006) and Carson (2002). Subramaniam, McManus and Zhang (2009) has suggested that the formation of such BOD sub-committees is systematically associated with organisational and corporate governance factors such as Board composition and leadership, ownership and organisational size.

Corporate Governance via Managerial Ownership

Jensen and Meckling (1976) had purported the convergence of interest model as a remedy towards the problems of agency theory whereby the information asymmetry and the divergence of conflicting interests between the owners and the management shall be eliminated if both are one and the same.

Jensen and Meckling (1976) argued that given that if the managers are also owners and their return on investments are affected by the decisions that they make concerning their organisations, the managers would act in the best interests of the organisation as a whole, thus, reducing the agency costs for their organisations.

A recent study conducted by Mustapha and Ahmad (2011) has found that managerial ownership has greatly reduced the monitoring costs and all other incidental agency costs for 867 public listed companies in Malaysia in 2006. This clearly supports the convergence of interest model as purported by Jensen and Meckling (1976).

An example of managerial ownership mechanisms being practised are performance linked remuneration for the Management, the use of Employees Share Option Schemes (ESOS) and bonuses in the form of share options.

Corporate Governance in Malaysia and Emerging Markets

Besides protecting the interest of shareholders, Corporate Governance has a signalling function to would-be investors; both domestic and foreign investors alike. Peters, Miller and Kusyk (2011) has argued that beside China, one of the main hindrances for firms from developed nations to enter emerging markets is that there is lack or absence of effective corporate governance and Corporate Social Responsibility (CSR) mechanisms. These mechanisms carry a great influence in building their confidence that their investments would be protected.

Unlike the West, in many developing economies such as Malaysia, many firms and private conglomerates in the East including emerging markets are controlled by families. This is evidenced by the keiretsus of Japan and the chaebols in South Korea. Even if there are movements towards having professionals in the governing boards, the members of the board themselves are often comprised of allies of the shareholders. Therefore, the corporate governance issues of premised on the principal-agency relationship but instead, a principal-principal issue is more prevalent if there are minority shareholders involved (Peters, Miller and Kusyk, 2011).

In the case of Malaysia and commonly in South East Asia, in addition to the existence of family controlled enterprises, the Government also have huge importance stakes in large corporations (including public listed ones). These corporations often referred to in Malaysia as Government-Linked Companies (GLCs) are held and controlled through various means (sometimes in combination of ways), including but not limited to the following:

i) Holding preferential ultimate veto rights or golden shares. This is normally held directly through the Government or through their investment arms such as Khazanah Nasional Berhad, Employees Provident Fund Board (EPF) or even Special Purpose Vehicles (SPVs) owned directly by the Ministry of Finance Incorporated (MOF Inc); or

ii) Vested powers to appoint Board members and the placement of Government representatives in the Board of Directors in the various strategic organisations;

iii) The final approval relating to the policy matters of the said organisations; and

iv) The indirect control over licenses and permits for the monopoly or near monopoly markets such as provision of electricity, defence or food.

La Porta *et al.* (2000) and Classens *et al.* (1999) has pointed out that the main problem of Corporate Governance in emerging markets have been due to the imbalance of power between controlling shareholders and minority shareholders.

In Malaysia, these imbalances between the powers of controlling shareholders and minorities for public companies listed on the local bourse (Bursa Malaysia Berhad) is counter balanced with the Minority Shareholder Watchdog Group (MSWG), a non-governmental organisation (NGO) setup in 2000 to protect the interests of minority shareholders through shareholders activism and it is funded by the Armed Forces Fund Board (Lembaga Tabung Angkatan Tentera), National Equity Corporation (Permodalan Nasional Berhad), Social Security Organisation (Pertubuhan Keselamatan Sosial or SOCSO) and the Pilgrimage Fund Board (Lembaga Tabung Haji).

Realising the foregoing, the Securities Commission (SC), the regulator of the securities and exchanges markets had on March 2000 released the Malaysian Code on Corporate Governance (the Code) to provide the road map of Corporate Governance in Malaysia. The Malaysian Code of Corporate Governance was revised in 2007 to empower the roles and responsibilities of the Board of Directors and the functions of their related sub-committees.

The Code was recently revised on March 2012 to strengthen the BOD structure and composition. The March 2012 Code is divided into eight (8) main principles of Corporate Governance as follows:

i)   **Principle 1:** Establish clear roles and responsibilities.
ii) **Principle 2:** Strengthen composition of the BOD
iii) **Principle 3:** Reinforce Independence
iv) **Principle 4:** Foster commitment
v)   **Principle 5:** Uphold integrity in financial reporting
vi) **Principle 6:** Recognise and manage risks
vii) **Principle 7:** Ensure timely and high quality disclosure
viii) **Principle 8:** Strengthen relationship between company and shareholders.

SC had also issue a separate Corporate Governance Blueprint in July 2011. The Blueprint has the objective of inculcating and promoting good compliance and instilling a Corporate Governance culture in Corporate Malaysia. The 2012 Code was part of the deliverables under the 2011 Corporate Governance Blueprint.

Corporate Governance in Islamic Banks

Corporate Governance deals with the methods and ways in which the providers of capital particularly shareholders assure themselves in ensuring the returns on their investment is optimised especially with the separation of the day to day management of their companies (Shleifer and Vishny, 1997).

Whilst, Corporate Governance entails so much more than mere supervision and control, Talamo (2011) argued that due to the dominant focus on the relationship between manager and shareholders and the structure and functions of the Board of Directors have partly distorted the actual definition of Corporate Governance.

According to the Islamic Development Bank, corporate governance embodies a blend of law, regulation, supervision and best practices from the private sector that enables the organisation to attract both financial and human capital to be able to perform efficiently and generate economic returns to its shareholders whilst safeguarding the interest of other stakeholders and the society as a whole (Islamic Development Bank, 2003).

Islamic banks like any other organisations is subjected to the normal internal corporate governance mechanisms including but not limited to Board Committees, external reporting standards, performance based rewards and policies and guidelines.

Being part of the financial system, Islamic Banks in Malaysia are also externally governed by the regulations and guidelines issued by the central bank, Bank Negara Malaysia, commonly referred to as BNM GPs (Garispanduan Bank Negara Malaysia). BNM's GP-1 for example, requires licensed financial institutions (including banks and insurance companies) to clearly demarcate the role of Chairman of Board of Directors with the Chief Executive Officer, minimising the effect of CEO duality on the effectiveness of Corporate Governance.

Very often the holding companies of the Islamic Banks in Malaysia are public companies listed on the Bursa Malaysia Berhad, the local bourse. Therefore, these companies are also bound by regulations set up by Bursa Malaysia such as the adherence to the Listing Requirements as well as the Practice Notes under the Malaysian Code on Takeovers and Mergers 2010 issued by the Securities Commissions.

However, unlike normal companies or banks, being a religious based organisation, Islamic Banks are also accountable and subjected to Shariah Governance. This feature is unique to Islamic Banks as the products and services rendered by the Islamic Banks must adhere to the tenets of Islamic Finance as well as ensuring that the underlying objectives of Islamic is not being undermined.

Shariah Governance for Islamic Financial Institutions (IFIs)

In addition to the common corporate governance structures, institutions or organisations subscribing to Islamic Finance, for it is derived from the divine revelation of Islamic tenets, has an extra dimension of governance in the form of Shariah Governance. Hassan (2011) has noted that the role of Shariah Governance exclusive and unique to the Islamic financial system management is a crucial portion of corporate governance for Islamic financial institutions.

In his recent studies on Shariah Governance, Hassan (2011) had also noted that Malaysia is a strong proponent of a regulation-based approach to Shariah governance system as compared to the Gulf Cooperation Council (GCC) member countries. Shariah governance in Islamic financial institutions is both regulated internally and externally. For internal shariah governance, the role is undertaken by the Shariah Board whilst externally, the Shariah Governance is done by adhering to external reporting requirements. The main feature of the internal Shariah Governance is the establishment of the Shariah Advisory Board or Shariah

Supervisory Board (SSB). The Accounting and Auditing Organisation for Islamic Financial Institutions (AOOIFI) has defined the SSB as follows:

"an independent body of specialised jurists in fiqh muamalat (Islamic commercial jurisprudence) that is entrusted with the duty of directing, reviewing and supervising the activities of the Islamic financial institutions in order to ensure that they are in compliance with the Islamic Shariah rules and principles."

Based on Ghayad (2008), the main role of Shariah Supervisory Board (SSB) is mainly to ensure that the operations and activities of the Islamic Banks conform to the principles of Islam and the products are Shariah compliant. The fatwas and rulings of the SSB shall be binding on the Islamic financial institutions. Therefore, it is interesting to note that since each Islamic Financial Institutions (IFI) has their own respective SSB, there is likelihood that the policy and procedures will indefinitely vary between IFIs.

However, at the point of writing, SSB's role in Islamic Banks is currently limited to the approval and review of the internal practices of that particular bank and the extent to which these SSB have an impact towards the overall Corporate Governance for that organisation is yet to be known and provides an interesting topic to venture into.

For externally Shariah governance, the IFIs are bound to follow the published several governance standards or directives issued by external regulatory bodies such as the AAOIFI, the Islamic Financial Services Board (IFSB), the Shariah Committee of central banks and regulators (e.g. the Shariah Advisory Panels of Bank Negara Malaysia and Securities Commission).

Capital Adequacy and Risk Capital Ratios

In short, capital adequacy is the measurement of the health of a financial institution and often reflected by the Risk Weighted Capital Adequacy Ratio (RWCAR).

As a barometer of financial health, the RWCAR indicates the level of capitalisation of a financial institution discounted against the risk undertaken for its daily business. Like any other unit of measurement, RWCAR is relative and therefore, need to be compared with the other financial institution in the same or similar market or environment. The following section will present the history of Basel Accord and the definition of Capital Adequacy before delving into detailed the ways of calculating the RWCAR.

Basel Accord and Capital Adequacy Requirements

In mid 1974, a private bank known as Herstatt Bank in Cologne, Germany was forced to close down by the German regulators as it no longer capitalised enough to meet its obligation. However, Herstatt Bank is involved in cross border transactions between Germany and the United States and the closure of the bank has caused settlement risks in international finance that has adverse impact on its counterpart banks in the United States.

Recognising the increasing globalisation of international banking and interdependency amongst financial institutions on the world scale, central bank governors of the Group of Ten (also known as G10 countries—Canada, France, Italy, Belgium, Japan, the Netherlands, United Kingdom and United States, Germany, Sweden and later joined by Switzerland) have set up an international forum or committee to share and discuss issues and extended cooperation on supervision and regulation of the banking industry in their respective countries.

The main aim of the committee is to provide a forum for regular cooperation to enhance the understanding of key supervisory issues and improve the quality of banking supervision worldwide (Bank for International Settlements, 2012). The committee, which was later known as Basel Committee on Banking Supervision (BSCS or simply referred to as Basel Committee) has its secretariat with the Bank of International Settlements (BIS). BIS is considered the central banks of central banks, acting as a central platform for international cooperation and standard setting for the global financial system.

The Basel Committee is responsible for the formulation of broad banking regulation and supervision guidelines and recommendations amongst its member-committees in areas such as capital risk, market risk and operational risks. These recommendations for regulations are documented as Basel Accord, which aims to ensure financial institutions are well capitalised to meet their obligations and absorb unexpected losses.

The Basel I Accord

In 1988, the Basel Committee has issued the first Basel Accord (commonly referred to Basel I), which focuses mainly on credit risks and the capitalisation of banks. Under Basel I, the Basel Committee has established as universal capital measurement system or yardstick in calculating the health of any financial institution in the world. The standard approach used was to assess the level of bank's capital as a percentage of the bank's loan assets based on a specified risk weighted approach.

Risk Weighted Assets (RWA)

The Basel Committee recognises that a bank's total loan portfolio consist of many various type of financial assets that carries different level of risks. Under Basel I, the Basel Committee has outlined the categorisation of banks assets and assigned the recommended level of risk weighting to those financial assets, as follows:

Table 2: Assignment of Risk Weighting under Basel I

Type of Bank Assets	Risk Weighting
Cash, central bank and government debt or any OECD	0%
Public sector debt	0%, 10%, 20% or 50% (optional)
Development Bank debt, OECD bank debt, OECD securities firm debt, non-OECD bank debt (under one year maturity) and non-OECD public sector debt, cash in collection	20%
Residential mortgages	50%
Private sector debt, non-OECD bank debt (maturing over a year), real estate, plant and equipment, capital instruments issued at other banks.	100%

As illustrated above, the higher the credit of a particular asset, the higher the risk weighting assigned to it. The first category which consists of cash and near cash sovereign guild edge credit is assigned a 0% rating. This is because the probability of those assets turning default is deemed (at least to the eyes of the Basel Committee), almost an impossibility.

A bank with 100% of its loan portfolio invested in pure cash or in debt instruments issued by OECD governments would have a zero risk weighting; implying that it has zero risk appetite and operating in a near risk free environment that would protect it from any banking risks. In the case of Malaysia, the Central Bank, Bank Negara Malaysia (BNM) has adapted the Basel I categorisation of banking assets to the Malaysian context in details and apportioned the risk weightings accordingly (Appendix 2).

Based on the above table, whilst the Bank discloses their financing assets at face value (net of any provision or impairment) in their respective Balance Sheet, the amount of the said long term asset might not be reflective of the true value of the asset from a RWCAR point of view. Therefore, the true value of the assets corresponds to the extent to which the amount advanced/sold/ purchased to the Customer or on behalf of the Customer is recoverable and be able to be re-circulated or re-ploughed to create the next financing asset.

In order to truly reflect the foregoing, each of the financing asset are categorised as per the type of assets mentioned above and discounted accordingly (Risk Discounting). The total financing assets of a particular Bank post risk discounting is referred to as the Risk Weighted Assets (RWA).

At every financial year end, each Bank licensed under the Acts governed by Bank Negara Malaysia are required to disclose the detailed computation of their RWA each year for juxtaposition with the RWA recorded the previous year. The RWA shall later be used as the denominator for the calculation of Risk Weighted Capital Adequacy Ratio (RWCAR).

Categorisation of Bank's Capital

Basel I has also categorised a bank's capital into several categories namely Tier 1, Tier 2 and Tier 3 Capitals as per the table below.

Table 3: Basel I Category of Bank's Capital (Bank of International Settlement, 2009)

Type of Capital	Basel Committee
Tier 1-Core Capital	This is the core capital of the Bank. This consists of the paid up capital, the disclosed accumulated reserves.
Tier 2	This supplementary capital raised by the Bank from several sources. Examples of Tier 2 capital are undisclosed reserves, revaluation reserves, hybrid financial instrument such as Irredeemable Convertible Bonds or perpetual Preference Shares and subordinated debt which ranks in claim lower than the depositors.
Tier 3	This is the type of capital that is raised by the Bank to eliminate their systematic business risks such as market risks, commodities risks and foreign currency risks. Examples of this type of capital are the capital apportioned for hedging, forward and futures contracts. However, for the calculation of capital adequacy ratio, Tier 3 capital is not included.

Tier 1 capital is the Core Capital of a particular bank where it consists of the crux of capital in the form of Shareholders' Paid Up Capital and accumulated retained earnings (Bank of International Settlement, 2009).

Tier 1 capital assumes a pure equity position whereby the returns of the Bank (if any) shall be accrued to the holders of Tier 1 capital in the form of undetermined dividend payout and/or in the increase in Net Tangible Asset (NTA) or value of the Bank.

Tier 2 on the other hand, is a quasi-equity capital whereby it consists of amount arising from the financial instruments or on-paper increase in value in addition to the core paid up amount captured under Tier 1 capital. The components of Tier 2 capital can be hybrid in nature whereby:

i)   It has elements of debt whereby the returns of such capital is fixed e.g. fixed dividend on Preference Shares or fixed cumulative coupon for Loan Stocks; and

ii) Elements of equity whereby the holder of the Tier 2 capital has a long term commitment with the Bank as the face value of the instrument would not be able to redeemed or cashed out due to the irredeemable and convertible features of that particular instrument. For example, Irredeemable Convertible Unsecured Loan Stocks (ICULS) is a Tier 2 capital since the ICULS holder is unable to retrieve/cash out their initial capital due to the Irredeemable feature and the ICULS is able to the converted into ordinary shares of the Bank due to its Convertible feature.

In the event of liquidation, Tier 2 and Tier 3 acts as buffer to Tier 1 capital; whereby as at the point of distress, any losses incurred by the Bank shall be absorbed by the Tier 3 and Tier 2 first, thus protecting the interest of the Tier 1 capital holders.

In order words, a particular Bank would still be able to continue its business provided that its Tier 1 capital has not been jeopardised. Once the Bank has suffered huge losses that eroded its Tier 1 capital, the Bank could be technically insolvent and consequently, risking the systematic risks of domino effects to other financial institutions and ultimately to the entire financial system itself.

Capital Ratios

In order to assess the level of healthiness of a bank, the Basel Committee has established the Capital Adequacy disclosure requirement. The Capital Adequacy is calculated in two (2) ways namely Core Capital Ratio and Risk Weighted Capital Adequacy Ratio (RWCAR).

The Core Capital Ratio (CCR) is simply Tier 1 Capital over its Risk Weighted Assets, as follows:

Core Capital Ratio (CCR) = Tier 1 Capital/Risk Weighted Assets

On the other hand, Risk Weighted Capital Adequacy Ratio (RWCAR) is calculated as follows:

RWCAR = (Tier 1 Capital + Tier 2 Capital)/Risk Weighted Assets.

The RWCAR is the bottom level of capitalisation of a bank and act as the first line of defence against accumulated losses of bank before the losses would start to deteriorate the core capital of the Bank.

As such, Basel I Accord has required banks to maintain a minimum RWCAR of 8% from its risk weighted assets. Bank Negara Malaysia (BNM), the central bank of Malaysia has adopted the Basel I Accord in 1989 and required banks to adhere to the 8% minimum RWCAR level.

On the onset, Basel I Accord has only covered credit risk relating to loan assets but has been expanded further to cover treasury market risk as well in 1996.

Subsequent Basel Accords (Basel II and Basel III)

The Basel I was later superseded by the much improved Basel II Accord in June 2004. BNM has adopted the Basel II Accord in two (2) stages; Standardised Approach in 2008 and the Internal Ratings Based (IRB) Approach in 2010.

Twenty years after the birth of the Basel Committee, in 2008, the world is faced with global financial crisis has threatened a system-wide failure to the global financial system. Huge international financial institutions such as Lehman Brothers, Northern Rock, Bear Stearns and AIG were not spared from the 2008 financial crisis.

Albeit the Basel Accords (I and II) have been assimilated and practised worldwide, it seems that the initiatives have not been effective enough to combat the possibility of bank runs and the lack of transparency in the financial markets (Carretta, Farina and Schwizer, 2010).

Three Pillars of Basel II

Unlike the previous Basel I accord which was mainly focussed on credit risks, the much improved Basel II in 2004 had further enhanced the quest for a more resilient banking system monitoring and regulation.

Basel II has widened the focus on three main areas; commonly referred to as "the Three Pillars" as better measurements of healthiness of a financial institution. The Three Pillars are namely:

i) **Pillar 1** deals with credit risks. Pillar 1 concentrates on realigning the minimum capital requirements with the actual risks involved in the daily operations of banks. The improvements in the minimum capital requirements are in the form of requiring higher levels of capital to commensurate with higher level of risks of bank financing activities and internal controls.

ii) **Pillar 2** deals with the role of the Supervisory Committee of the Central Bank. This Committee shall be responsible in overseeing the activities and risk profiles of banks and advises the Board of Directors of those banks whether the minimum capital requirements are sufficient or needed to be increased and also provide consultancy as to whether remedial actions are needed.

iii) **Pillar 3** engages on market discipline whereby the Basel Committee has outlined the standards of which Banks are to adhere in order to provide transparency of reporting to the stakeholders.

Basel II has also provided that under Pillar 1 (Credit Risk), there are two (2) different approaches to be used, namely Standardised Approach and Internal Rating Based (IRB) Approach. The Standardised Approach is similar to the provisions under Basel I whilst the IRB approach is a risk based approach whereby the risk weighting for each asset is based on Value at Risk (VAR) methodologies whereby its assigned credit risk components namely Probability of Default (PD), Loss Given Default (LGD) and Expected Loss (EL) or sometimes referred to as Exposure at Default (EAD) (Capital Adequacy Framework for Islamic Banks, Bank Negara Malaysia, 2012).

PD assigns the probability of event of default occurring for the financing asset, the LGD estimates the degree the Bank is able to recover the amount financed (including foreclosure any security attached) and EL estimates the percentage of actual residual loss of which the Bank would ultimately suffer in the event the financing assets goes bad.

All the credit risk measures are ranked and the risk weighting are assigned based on the final ranking which is a combination of the three foregoing measures. The IRB approach is voluntary and each Bank is free to assign the risk weightings based on their financing portfolio.

In response to the 2008 global financial crisis, the Basel Committee has in 2010, released the latest Basel III in with more stringent capital adequacy requirements (*The Basel Accord and Capital Requirements Directive,* United Kingdom Financial Services Authority, http://www.fsa.gov.uk/about/what/international/basel).

Implementation of Basel III Accords in Malaysia

In December 2011, BNM has iterated that it will start to adopt the Basel III and every bank in Malaysia is required to provide their Basel III disclosure in addition to their normal financial statements by 2013.

What do we know about Islamic Finance or Islamic Banking

The section shall delved into previous studies conducted on Islamic Finance and Banking with specific attention to the risk behaviours of Islamic Banks and the Capital Adequacy Framework for Islamic Bank (CAFIB), Islamic equivalent of the Basel Accord, duly customised and assimilated by Bank Negara Malaysia in tandem with the spirit and principle under the Basel Accords.

Islamic Finance Mechanisms and Risk Behaviours

Arzu *et al.* (2005) has clearly identified two main categories of risk behaviours: risk taker who are willing to accept higher risks for higher returns and risk averse individuals accept lower levels of risks for lower returns.

By virtue of being a partner, the Islamic financial institution on the onset, assumes equity risks and therefore, would have to assume the risk weighting similar to common shareholders. This view is supported by Alexakis and Tsikouras (2009) which defended that Islamic Finance is an asset based system whereby money has no intrinsic value and ethical and social aspects and speculative behaviours such as gambling and taking excessive risk is prohibited.

Rosly and Zaini (2008) argued that Islamic finance should have positive impact towards risk since Islam forces its practitioners to assume equity risks in a calculated way since avoiding risk in Islam is only allowed when there is no promise of contractual income.

Nevertherless, Rosly and Zaini (2008) has also argued that Islamic banking in Malaysia may not be able to find its competitive advantage in profit-sharing or commercial ventures as stipulated under the pretext of al-bay.

The study conducted by Rosli and Zaini (2008) on deposits mobilisation has suggested that in the context of Islamic banks in Malaysia, the advantages of trade based and profit and loss sharing (PLS) contracts under Islamic Finance are not fully materialised since these contracts are mere rebranding of existing conventional banking products.

However, more recent studies (post 2008 financial crisis) by both Chazi and Syed (2010) and Ahmed (2010) have argued that Islamic banks globally were able to weather the adverse effects from the financial crisis in 2008 due to the risk aversion mechanisms inherent in basic Islamic finance principles such as prohibition of riba' and gambling, concept of social justice and no reward without risk (*al ghonm-bil ghorm*).

This view is then further supported by Tahir and Brimble (2011) that explored on investment behaviours of a group of Muslims which suggested that the degree of religiosity of an individual does influence their investment behaviour and there is an element of wealth maximisation to Islamic investment decisions.

Tahir and Bramble (2011) also observed that there is evidence of wealth-maximisation behaviours amongst Muslim investors and Islamic investors consider other factors in addition to risk, rate of return and religious orientations.

Relevance of Risk Based Capital Ratio for Islamic Banks

Ahmed (1994) and El-Ghazali (1994) and duly concurred by Khan and Bhatti (2008) have argued that Islamic finance particularly Islamic Banking is an equity based system and does not subscribe to the conventional funding criteria such as creditworthiness and strong collateral as basis for financing. In their own opinions, Islamic Banking financings are based on merits in more equitable allocation and distribution of wealth and resources instead of purely based on credit and collateral. Therefore, good projects with good resources allocation prospects but weak collateral are preferred to a project with better collateral but wasteful, superfluous and unproductive.

In its purest form, an Islamic Bank working on a pure Profit and Loss Sharing (PLS) scheme only, mainly due to its equity-like nature, does not require a capital adequacy mechanism. This is because Islamic Finance does not work in similar ways as conventional finance whereby the former takes on a more trading partner approach to its clients compared to the typical lender-borrower approach of conventional financing. By virtue of being a partner, the Islamic financial institution on the onset, assumes equity risks and therefore, would have to assume the risk weighting similar to common shareholders (Archer, Abdel Karim and Sundararajan (2010).

Under the aforementioned BNM's adaptation of the Basel Accord, a pure Islamic bank would have to assign 100% risk weighting to all its financing assets, thus, rendering the Islamic bank to have very low RWCAR compared their conventional banking counterparts. This would imply that any Islamic bank would be the least capitalised banks in the world; consequently, reducing their ratings and the subsequently, the required rate of returns by their investors.

However, Abdel Karim (2006) has also argued the opposite. For example, since the customers of PLS accounts or Profit or Loss Sharing Investment Accounts (PSIA) holders are (by virtue of its unique nature) shareholders, PSIA holders bear their own commercial risks and thus, should not attract any capital charges. This is because the PSIA stands in the same shoes of the IFIs, and thus willingly assumes the same level of risks.

The above two differing scenarios clearly showed that the direct adoption or adaptation of the Basel Accord would not give the true and fair view of the capitalisation strength of the Islamic bank and would make comparisons with their conventional counterparties unreliable.

Alexakis and Tsikouras (2009) also agreed that due to the nature of operations of Islamic banks, adjustments to the Basel Accord are necessary. Given that the products introduced by Islamic Banks are not only confined to PLS based contracts but also sale based (bai') contracts such as Murabahah, Bai' Istisna' whereby the risks are not straightforward lender-borrower relationship, the various structures that exist under different Islamic contracts would attract different type of risks at different stages of the contract.

Amongst the risks that are identified under Islamic financial contracts include but not limited to the credit risks, market risks and commercial risks (for sales based contracts), fiduciary risks (for contracts that requires agency such as Mudharabah and Wakalah) and performance risks (for contracts such as Bai' Salam and Bai' Istisna').

The view is also shared by the AAOIFI and Islamic Finance Services Board (IFSB) and in response, the AAOIFI had in 1999 published the Statement on the Purpose and Calculation of the Capital Adequacy Ratio (CAR) for Islamic Banks and IFSB has developed the Capital Adequacy Standards for Institutions (other than Insurance Institutions) (CAS) in 2005 which has took effect in 2007.

Abdel Karim (2006) has outlined his findings on the salient features of the CAS are as follows:

i) The CAS has taken specific characteristics of IFIs and the standard is complementary to Pillar 1 of Basel II;

ii) CAS has taken the approach of investor protection when dealing with Profit and Loss Sharing Investment Accounts (PSIA). Therefore, although PSIA holders bear their own commercial risks, some capital are still needed to be set aside to cater for the credit and market risks. AAOIFI has earlier proposed the 50% risk weighting for PISA and the CAS has assigned a more flexible risk weighting;

iii) The CAS has made provisions for specific issues that are peculiar to Shariah compliant/Shariah based products which are not addressed by the Basel accord.

Capital Adequacy Framework for Islamic Banks (CAFIB)

With the awakening of the 2008 global financial crisis and the need to have a standardised approach in assessing the health of financial institutions across the board, the Central Bank of Malaysia, had on 1 January 2008, developed the Capital Adequacy Framework for Islamic Banks (CAFIB) by referencing the said framework to the previous works done by the Islamic Financial Services Board (IFSB) (Clause 1.4, Part A.1 Executive Summary, Capital Adequacy Framework for Islamic Banks (CAFIB), Bank Negara Malaysia (BNM/RH/GL002-14), 2010).

CAFIB assimilates all three pillars under the Basel II Accords and subsequently, uses similar approaches to the risk categories as follows:

Table 4: CAFIB's Assimilation of Basel II 3 Pillars

No.	Risk Type	Available Approaches
1	Credit Risk	• Standardised Approach • Internal Rating Based (IRB) Approach
2	Market Risk	• Standardised Approach • Internal Models Approach (IMA)
3	Operational Risk	• Basic Indicator Approach (BIA) • Standardised Approach (TSA) • Alternative Standardised Approach (ASA)

The study shall only delve briefly into the CAFIB's Credit Risk weighting assignment methodology. This is due to the vast details of CAFIB's framework in assigning and computing the risk weightings.

CAFIB-Credit Risk

There are two main methods in approaching Credit Risk by assigning the risk weighting and capital requirements under CAFIB, namely using the Standardised Approach (SA) and the Internal Rating Based (IRB) Approach. CAFIB has provided the flexibility for Islamic Banks in Malaysia to use either one of the approaches.

The Standard Approach basically refers to predefined risk weighting based on set of exposures or class of assets as determined in the CAFIB Framework. Under the Standard Approach, the risk weighting is assigned based on the ratings provided by the external credit assessment institutions (ECAI) such as Standard and Poor's (S&P), Fitch, Moody's, Rating Agency of Malaysia (RAM) and the Malaysian Rating Corporation Berhad (MARC).

On the other hand, the IRB approach, each Islamic Bank shall use their own internal rating systems, based on the Value at Risk (VAR) methodology in measuring credit risks and assigns the risk weighted based on the resultant composite Probability of Default (PD), Loss Given Default (LGD) and Exposure at Default (EAD) ratings (Clause 2.7, Capital Adequacy Framework for Islamic Banks, BNM, 2010).

Islamic Bank Risk Based Capital Ratios

Chazi and Syed (2010) derived their methodology from Estrella *et al.* (2000) in their study has focused on three (3) major risk based capital ratios, namely:

i) Leverage Ratios;
   = Tier 1 capital/Total Tangible Assets
ii) Gross Revenue Ratios;
   = Tier 1 capital/Total Revenue (interest and non interest income before expense)
iii) Risk Weighted Capital Adequacy Ratios (RWCAR).
   = Tier 1 capital/Risk Weighted Assets

Chazi and Syed (2010) also made comparisons between liquidity and profitability ratios between Islamic Bank and conventional banks in their sample of 27 Islamic Banks and 27 Conventional Banks from 14 countries such as Bangladesh, Bahrain, Britain, Egypt, Indonesia, Kuwait, Malaysia, Pakistan, Qatar, Kingdom of Saudi Arabia, Turkey, United Arab Emirates (UAE) and Yemen.

The approach undertaken by Chazi and Syed (2010) is a much simplistic version compared to the measurements purported by the Basel Committee, AAOIFI, IFSB or CAFIB. The calculation by

Chazi and Syed (2010) is only as per Basel I level and does not include the other 2 pillars as per Basel II requirements.

Furthermore, Chazi & Syed (2010) has not taken Tier 2 capital into consideration as Islamic banks running on pure Islamic finance principals does not conform to the normal conventional banking (which creates money from money) and therefore does not account for any debt based capital which qualifies under Tier 2 capital.

However, for the purpose of this study, both the Core Capital Ratio (CCR) and RWCAR (as per the amount disclosed in the financial statements) shall be observed.

Conceptual Framework

For the purpose of this research, there are three (3) main variables namely Corporate Governance (CG), Firm Characteristics (FC) and Risk Weighted Capital Adequacy Ratio (RWCAR).

Based on the foregoing, the conceptual framework for this research is as follows:

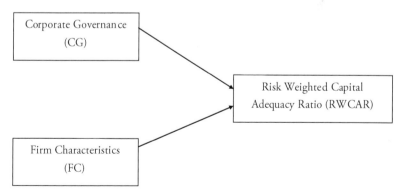

Whereby there is a relationship between components of Corporate Governance (CG) and Firm Characteristics (FC) and Risk Weighted Capital Adequacy Ratio (RWCAR).

Drivers of Corporate Governance

Several studies namely Khanchel (2007), Subramaniam, McManus and Zhang (2009) and Caretta, Farina and Schweizer (2010) have identified the drivers of Corporate Governance (in no particular order of importance) as follows:

i) BOD sizes;
ii) Board composition (executive vs non executive directors) (Independent Directors vs Non Independent Directors);
iii) CEO duality (the split between role of Chairman and Chief Executive Officer (CEO));
iv) Frequency of BOD meetings.

Whilst most of them agree on the above, several other constructs were separately suggested as the drivers of Corporate Governance (either internal or external to the firm) as follows:

Table 5: Drivers of Corporate Governance

Other Drivers of Corporate Governance	Details	Sources
Auditors Reputation	The selection and appointment of reputable auditors may signals that the disclosure made is more accurate and representative of the organisation being audited. This is because, post Enron ordeal, auditors are more cautious and wary of their professionalism and reputational risk that they would face if unscrupulous practices is to be allowed.	Subramaniam, McManus & Zhang (2009)

Other Drivers of Corporate Governance	Details	Sources
Industry Type	Some industries are riskier than others and therefore, would be more likely to adopt and subjected to Corporate Governance practices, rules and regulations.	Subramaniam, McManus & Zhang (2009)
CEO Duality	CEO is the key person for Management and a CEO dominated BOD is likely to exist if the CEO and the Chairman of the BOD is the same person. Bliss, Muniandy & Majid (2007) has argued that this CEO Duality is to be more likely associated with ineffective monitoring control systems due to imbalance of power and lack of check and balance mechanism between the BOD and the Management.	Bliss, Muniandy & Majid (2007), BNM GP1-i, Bank Negara Malaysia.
Organisational Complexity	Organisations increase in complexity as it grows bigger and involves in various activities across different industries. High level of organisational complexity requires higher level of monitoring and agency costs and is more likely to undermine effective Corporate Governance practices.	Subramaniam, McManus & Zhang (2009)
Financial Reporting risks	Companies with huge portion of current assets that are subjected to manipulation of accounting treatment such as account receivables and inventory are	

Other Drivers of Corporate Governance	Details	Sources
	expected to have a high degree of Financial Reporting risks, which in the end provides avenue for information asymmetry, which in turn, undermines the effectiveness of Corporate Governance.	Subramaniam, McManus & Zhang (2009)
Leverage	Highly geared companies are often more risky and subjected to covenants from lenders and stakeholders which require a higher level of internal monitoring and controls system, which positively increase Corporate Governance.	Subramaniam, McManus & Zhang (2009)
Directors' incentive schemes	The view that the Directors are acting for the benefit of shareholders and thus, must be compensated commensurably and failure to link their remunerations to their performance might lead to counter effective actions that might detriment the interest of shareholders. However, such remuneration packages need to be well designed to prevent the directors neglecting interests of other non-shareholders stakeholders. This is also supported by the Basel Committee in their recommendation in 2005.	Caretta, Farina & Schweizer (2010)

Other Drivers of Corporate Governance	Details	Sources
Management Information System	The BOD sets the direction of the organisation, which will be carried out by the Management on the daily basis. An advance management information system is required to enable free flow of data on the operational level to the strategic level up to the BOD level to ensure coherence and conformity to enable effective Corporate Governance.	Caretta, Farina & Schweizer (2010)

However, due to the nature of the Islamic banking in Malaysia, all the drivers as per the table above shall not be taken into account. This is because:

i) Given the nature of the industry that is relatively small, banks (including Islamic banks) in Malaysia only employs the Big Four accounting firms and thus, the reputation of the auditors is perceived not to be a significant driver to CG;

ii) As the study relates to the same industry in the same country offering similar products, all the Islamic banks are bound with the same regulations for disclosure and organisational complexity;

iii) Bank Negara Malaysia's regulation under the Guidelines on Corporate Governance for Licensed Islamic Banks (GP1-i) has prompted all financial institutions to separate the functions of the Chairman of the Board of Directors and the Chief Executive Officer;

iv) Whilst the study also recognises that even the separation of roles, the CEO might still be influential enough to steer the decision of the Board of Directors, but however, this information is subjective and might not be readily available to the public;

v) Variables such as directors' incentive schemes and management information systems are internal information that whilst expected to vary tremendously across the industry, such information are often not reflected entirely in the annual report.

vi) Furthermore, given that the study is conducted over a period of time after the 2008 global financial crisis, the Islamic Banks might not be expensing on as much on the two items and if they do, they might not be doing it each and every year, thus, negate the need for the variables to be considered.

Firm Characteristics (FC)

As outlined previously, unlike Corporate Governance, firm characteristics are more diverse as it entails everything that describes the particular organisation.

However, as a subject matter towards disclosure and corporate governance, based on the literature, several scholars namely Aripin, Tower and Taylor (2011) in their studies on financial disclosure of firms in Australia have given insights on several key drivers of firm characteristics, namely:

i)   Firm size; and
ii) Concentration of ownership.

Aripin, Tower and Taylor (2011) have argued that concentrated of ownership reduces the effects from agency problem and partly negates the need for external disclosure. This approach especially on concentration of ownership is also shared by Peters, Miller and Kusyk (2011) in their studies on corporate governance and corporate social responsibility in emerging markets. In their studies, they have noted that in developing countries, the potential conflicts of interests does not rise between shareholders and managers (to the same extent of developed nations) but between majority and minority shareholders. This is due to the fact that most firms in the emerging markets are family owned or controlled and thus, rendering the amalgamation of owners and managers.

However, the second dimension (i.e. concentration of ownership) needed to be modified to suit the scope of the study. This is due to the fact that, most if not all the full-fledged Islamic banks in Malaysia are subsidiaries of a bigger financial group and normally 100% owned by the ultimate holding company of the financial group.

Nevertheless, due to the liberalisation stance taken by the Central Bank (Bank Negara Malaysia) in recent years, it is interesting to note that many foreign-owned banks to incorporate their Islamic banking subsidiaries in Malaysia e.g. Kuwait Finance House (which is fully foreign owned via the Kuwait Finance House of Kuwait) or even taking shareholding stake in the existing local Islamic banks listed on the Bursa Malaysia (Malaysia Bourse) e.g. Dubai Banking Group's (DBG) 30.5% interest in Bank Islam Malaysia Berhad.

Therefore, based on the foregoing recent development in the Malaysian Islamic banking industry, the 2nd item shall be remodelled as follows:

i)   Concentration of foreign ownership in the Islamic bank.

Hypotheses Development

Hypothesis 1:

Bigger BOD sizes increases the diversity of collective knowledge experience of the collective BOD and at the same time, reduces collectivism which hinders effective decision making, which in turn, might contribute to lower level of riskiness of financing assets; which will effectively improve RWCAR.

The studies made by Pathan (2008) on large US Banks from the period of 1997 to 2004 revealed that strong Boards characterised by small and less restrictive positively affect the risk taking behaviour of Banks in the US. Therefore, the bigger the BOD size, the lower risk taking behaviour is expected and thus, RWCAR is expected to increase.

H1: BOD sizes has a positive relationship with RWCAR of Islamic Banks in Malaysia (BODSIZE)

Hypothesis 2:

The higher ratio of Non Executive Directors balances the power in the BOD and increase independence of the BOD. This is expected to lead to better risk management of financing assets thus, reduces the RWCAR.

Lappalainen and Niskanen (2012) had vide their research on SMEs in Finland had found that ownership structure and Board composition are significant determinants of firm performance. Wagner et al (1998) has argued that BOD comprises of members from outside the organisation should be generally superior to the BOD consist of insiders i.e executive directors.

Subramaniam, McManus and Zhang (2009) has argued that independent and non-executive directors tend to be more concerned on their reputation and thus, provides a better quality governance structure.

H2: Ratio between Executive and Non-Executive Directors has negative relationship with RWCAR of Islamic Banks in Malaysia (EXECRATIO).

Hypothesis 3:

The results of empirical studies on the role of Independent and Non Independent Directors on firm performance and risk management are mixed. Some prior works such as Yermack (1996), Dalton et al (1999) and de Andres et al (2005) have failed to establish the link between outside directors with the performance of firms.

On the other hand, Brennan (2006) has argued that the extent to which corporate governance has an impact on firm performance varies according to countries and jurisdictions and cross-country research can provide valuable incremental insights. Likewise, Lappalainen & Niskanen (2012) had done their research on SMEs in Finland and found that ownership structure and Board composition are significant determinants of firm performance.

Subramaniam, McManus & Zhang (2009) has argued that independent and non-executive directors tend to be more concerned on their reputation and thus, provides a better quality governance structure. Therefore, it is expected that an Islamic bank with a higher percentage of Independent Directors would effectively improve decision making and thus, register a better RWCAR.

H3: Ratio between Independent and Non-Independent Directors has positive relationship with RWCAR of Islamic Banks in Malaysia (INDPRATIO)

Hypothesis 4:

Information asymmetry is likely to be minimised if the information is channelled up to the BOD on a more accurate and timely basis. Therefore, it is expected that the frequency of BOD meeting would enable better control and monitoring of the Islamic Banks, thus improving the RWCAR. This is well supported by Shivdasani & Zenner (2004) who argued that the frequency of BOD meetings is factor of the need of higher supervision and control. This is also supported by Khancel (2007) in his studies has argued that the frequency of BOD meetings increase the recovery from poor performance.

H4: Frequency of BOD meeting has positive relationship with RWCAR of Islamic Banks in Malaysia (FREQBOD).

Hypothesis 5:

Aripin and Taylor (2011) has argued that firm size has positive relationship with the financial ratio disclosure practices in public listed firms in Australia. Chau and Gray (2002) and Patelli & Prencipe (2007) have both argued that firm size influences voluntary financial reporting practices in firms. Therefore, since RWCAR is a form of financial reporting, it is expected that firm size would have a positive correlation with RWCAR of Islamic Banks in Malaysia.

H5: Total Assets has positive relationship with RWCAR of Islamic Banks in Malaysia (TASSETS).

Hypothesis 6:

Aripin & Taylor (2011) have argued that firm size influences the financial ratio disclosure practices in firms. Chau and Gray (2002) and Patelli & Prencipe (2007) have both argued that firm size influences voluntary financial reporting practices in firms. Therefore, since RWCAR is a form of financial reporting, it is expected that firm size would have a positive correlation with RWCAR of Islamic Banks in Malaysia.

Islamic Banks' total assets consists of many item including properties, placements of deposits in other financial institutions, financing and advances and statutory deposit with Bank Negara Malaysia. However, this variable of Total Financing Assets is the more precise indicator of risk adverseness of a particular Islamic

Bank as it is the least liquid of the financial assets and it has the most element of credit risk, Pillar 1 of the Basel Accord. Due to the foregoing, this variable is included in the study.

H6: Total Financing Assets has positive correlation with RWCAR of Islamic Banks in Malaysia (FINASSETS)

Hypothesis 7:

As mentioned, ownership structure and Board composition are significant determinants of firm performance (Lappalainen & Niskanen, 2012). Also, ownership concentration will reduce agency but at the expense of increasing risk aversion. Che Haat, Abdul Rahman & Mahenthiran (2008) in their studies on corporate governance, transparency and performance of Malaysian companies have found that foreign ownership as one of the most significant predictors of market performance on public listed companies in Malaysia. Therefore, it is expected that foreign ownership would increase risk aversion, leading to a better management of financing assets of Islamic Banks, which in turn, lower the risk discounting and thus, better RWCAR.

H7: Foreign ownership has positive correlation with RWCAR of Islamic Banks in Malaysia (FOREOWN).

Subsequently, based on the existing work done on the constructs, the following summarized the hypotheses.

Table 6: Summary of hypotheses

No.	Hypothesis
H1	BOD sizes (BODSIZE) has a positive relationship with RWCAR of Islamic Banks in Malaysia.
H2	Ratio between Executive and Non-Executive Directors (EXECRATIO) has negative relationship with RWCAR of Islamic Banks in Malaysia.
H3	Ratio between Independent and Non-Independent Directors (INDPRATIO) has positive relationship with RWCAR of Islamic Banks in Malaysia.
H4	Frequency of BOD meeting (FREQBOD) has positive relationship with RWCAR of Islamic Banks in Malaysia.
H5	Total Assets (TASSETS) has positive relationship with RWCAR of Islamic Banks in Malaysia.
H6	Total Financing Assets (FINASSETS) has positive relationship with RWCAR of Islamic Banks in Malaysia.
H7	Foreign ownership (FOREOWN) has positive relationship with RWCAR of Islamic Banks in Malaysia.

Weathering the Global Crisis

Overall Findings-Relationship Roadmap

Based on the foregoing PMCC results, the roadmap of relationships between the variables including the components of RWCAR such as TIER1, CORECAP and RWA is depicted in a simplified manner as per Diagram 1 below.

As a basis to simplify the diagram, any PMCC score below 0.30 is considered weak and therefore, eliminated from the diagram.

Diagram 4.1: Correlation Roadmap

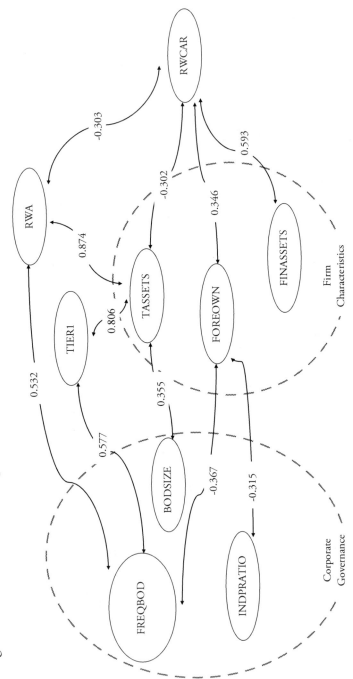

Findings from Correlation Roadmap

Based on the simplified correlation roadmap, a few interesting findings are observed from the study:

i) The variable EXECRATIO is missing. EXECRATIO has a negative correlation of 0.253 based on 95% confidence level but was not included in the roadmap since the relationship is considered weak as it is below 0.3. Therefore, it can be deduced that the ratio of Executive Directors against Non Executive Directors in the BOD does not seemed to be in any remote way related to RWCAR.

ii) Firm Characteristics (FC) variables such as FOREOWN, TASSETS and FINASSETS are directly linked to RWCAR whilst none of the Corporate Governance variables are connected.

Some CG variables such as FREQBOD however, do correlate to RWCAR via FC variables such as FOREOWN and TASSETS (via TIER1 route). However, this is highly inconclusive as the PMCC only measures the strength of relationship between the variables and level of influence CG variables to FC variables. This could be used as a platform for further research in the future.

iii) Although TIER1 is a component of RWCAR, that particular variable is found not to be correlated to RWCAR but FINASSETS which makes part of RWA (without risk discounting) is found to be positively correlated to RWCAR.

On the onset, the study has the objective of quantifying the strength of the relationships between corporate governance and firm characteristics (which are both considered western based concepts) by looking into information obtained from the financial statements of the Islamic Banks in Malaysia after the 2008 global financial crisis.

Based on previous studies conducted on Corporate Governance, Firm Characteristics, Islamic Finance and Risk Weighted Capital Adequacy Ratio, the following hypotheses were made and the secondary data was observed. The conclusion from the study is depicted as follows:

Table 7: Summary of Hypothesis and Result from Study

No.	Hypothesis	Result from Study
H1	BOD sizes (BODSIZE) has a **positive relationship** with RWCAR of Islamic Banks in Malaysia.	Hypothesis rejected.
H2	Ratio between Executive and Non-Executive Directors (EXECRATIO) has **negative relationship** with RWCAR of Islamic Banks in Malaysia.	Hypothesis rejected.
H3	Ratio between Independent and Non-Independent Directors (INDPRATIO) has **positive relationship** with RWCAR of Islamic Banks in Malaysia.	Hypothesis rejected.
H4	Frequency of BOD meeting (FREQBOD) has positive relationship with RWCAR of Islamic Banks in Malaysia.	Hypothesis rejected.
H5	Total Assets (TASSETS) has positive relationship with RWCAR of Islamic Banks in Malaysia.	Hypothesis rejected.
H6	Total Financing Assets (FINASSETS) has positive relationship with RWCAR of Islamic Banks in Malaysia.	Hypothesis accepted.
H7	Foreign ownership (FOREOWN) has positive relationship with RWCAR of Islamic Banks in Malaysia.	Hypothesis accepted.

The relationship between the CG and FC variables with RWCAR is depicted clearly in Diagram 4.1. From the diagram, it is certain that FINASSETS and FOREOWN have positive strong relationship with RWCAR.

It is noted from the same diagram that albeit FREQBOD does not have strong relationship with RWCAR, it has strong positive relationships with TIER1 and RWA and a strong negative relationship with FOREOWN. Since TIER1 and RWA are components of RWCAR and FOREOWN has a strong positive relationship with RWCAR, this might suggest that albeit FREQBOD, a CG variable has an indirect relationship to RWCAR through those foregoing variables.

Discussion on the findings

Since 2006, there has been a mushrooming of Islamic Banks in the Malaysian Financial Market with some are direct subsidiaries of foreign banks such as Kuwait Finance House, Al Rajhi Bank and Asian Finance Bank Berhad.

The 2008 global financial crisis which started in the United States have posed a systematic threat to the global financial systems. Due to the mortgage subprime issue in the US, other economies such as UK, Europe and Dubai were directly affected as funds were pulled out of those countries to beef up and recapitalised the Banks. This led to the domino effects on the Eurozone, which caused several countries such as Spain, Portugal, Iceland and Greece, to name a few, still suffer even 3 years after the crisis swarmed over the US. Even at the point of writing, the Eurozone has not fully recovered.

This phenomenon is not new. Banking related financial crisis was prevalent in the recent 1998 Asian Financial Crisis, barely 10 years prior to the one in the US. Despite having the Basel Accord in place which was supposedly ensuring the Banks have enough capitalisations, mere disclosure to regulation failed to prevent the crisis from happening.

In order to avoid such things from happening, regulators realised that regulation alone might not be enough. After all, policies and guidelines will remain so unless being effectively implemented in the Banks. Hence, they often turn to Corporate Governance as a supplement to their regulatory diet and consequently, one would expect that Corporate Governance, not Firm Characteristics would dictate Banks to be 'risk healthy' with high RWCAR.

Islamic Banks on the other hand, on the theoretical level, operates much differently from conventional banks whereby the underlying relationship between the Bank and the client is based on the fundamentals of partnership and/or trading partners unlike the normal Lender-Borrower relationship of conventional banks. Therefore, it is presumed that with its riskier approach to financing, these Islamic banks would fare lesser in terms of its RWCAR and thus, more susceptible to the systemic failures. However, this was proven wrong by Chazi & Syed (2010) when their research revealed Islamic banks were shielded from the adverse effects of the financial meltdown in the West.

It is quite a revelation to the authors that none of the Corporate Governance variables were found to be significant enough to be correlated to the RWCARs recorded but rather Firm Characteristics (FC) variables have more prevalent significance when it comes to RWCAR. A possible reason is the fact that the study conducted was only limited to the Malaysian Islamic Banks which operated as full-fledged banks offering similar across the board Shariah based financial products and services. The Malaysian Islamic Banks, although differ in terms of sizes, capitalisation, size of their Board of Directors and so forth, still subjected to the same regulations by regulatory bodies such as Bank Negara Malaysia and the Securities Commission. Therefore, the lack of variety or rather the high degree of uniformity of governance structure might have caused the study unable to fully reach its desired goals.

Implications

The study conducted has shown the light on the relationship of Corporate Governance and Firm Characteristics with RWCAR, namely:

i) Firm Characteristics have quite strong relationship with RWCA whereby Total Assets has a negative relationship and Foreign Ownership has a positive relationship with RWCAR;

ii) There is no relationship between Corporate Governance (CG) and Risk Weighted Capital Adequacy Ratio (RWCAR);

iii) Some CG variables such as FREQBOD however, do correlate to RWCAR via FC variables such as FOREOWN and TASSETS (via TIER1 route). This signals that FREQBOD might have an indirect relationship and FOREOWN, TASSETS and TIER1 might be intermediate variables linking FREQBOD and RWCAR.

For regulators of the financial industries such as Bank Negara Malaysia or Securities Commission, the above observations made from the study might suggest the following:

i) Since CG variables do not have direct relationship with RWCAR and the fact that banking industry is a highly regulated industry, regulators might need to seek other areas to install control mechanisms apart from the empowerment of the BOD and BOD structure. Since FOREOWN has a strong correlation with RWCAR, regulator might consider more liberalisation in regulation level of foreign ownership or setting limits on concentration of effective shareholding as a way to increase the quality of Islamic Banks in Malaysia; which in turn, increases the quality profile of Malaysian corporations on the global scale.

ii) Since FOREOWN has positive relationship with RWCAR, regulators such as Securities Commission might look into the shareholding issues such as unfair treatment to minority shareholders or even increasing the flexibility of managerial ownership to ensure diversity of shareholdings structure; which might an effective tool in increase the RWCAR of Islamic Banks in Malaysia.

iii) Since FINASSETS has a positive relationship with RWCAR, this suggests that as the Total Financing Assets of the Islamic Bank grows, RWCAR is expected to increase as well. Given that in the short term, TIER1 capital is unlikely to change, the increase in Total Financing Assets could also cause the denominator (i.e. the Risk Weighted Assets) to decrease.

This could imply two possible scenarios. Firstly, further scrutiny on the Internal Rating Based (IRB) approaches needed to be made. This is because the regulation currently allows for the Islamic Banks to assign their risk weighting based on their own Internal Rating System. The regulator could use this study as a basis to conduct further investigation and assess whether the IRB approach taken by the Islamic Bank is exhaustive and accurate enough to assign the correct risk weighting and whether the industry needs to have a standard IRB approach and amend and update the CAFIB accordingly.

Secondly, the study seems to imply that as Islamic Banks grows in assets, there is more leeway for that Islamic Banks to take on more risky assets. Therefore, regulators such as BNM might need to impose more conservative the risk weightings or impose higher minimum RWCAR level as ways to improve the quality of Islamic Banks in Malaysia.

For the Islamic Banks themselves, since FREQBOD is seen to have positive relationship with TIER1 and RWA (which are the critical components to RWCAR) the study could be used to assess the whether a more proactive by way of more frequent BOD meeting might be as useful way in ensuring indirect control over RWCAR. Although previous studies are divided on frequency of BOD meeting as an effective tool to firm's performance, in the case of Islamic Banks in Malaysia, a more frequent BOD meeting might be an effective tools to ensure the quality of Islamic Banks in terms of maintaining asset quality.

Directions for further research

The study however, was not without its shortcomings. It was only limited to the Malaysian Islamic Banks which operated as full-fledged banks offering across the board Shariah based financial products and services. The Malaysian Islamic Banks, although differ in terms of sizes, capitalisation, size of their Board of Directors and so forth, still subjected to the same regulations by regulatory bodies such as Bank Negara Malaysia and the Securities Commission. Therefore, the lack of variety or rather the high degree of uniformity of governance structure might have caused the study unable to fully reach its desired goals. The study would be further improved if the scope of coverage is extended to the neighbouring countries which also practices Islamic banking and finance such as Singapore, Indonesia and Brunei.

The Islamic banking industry in Malaysia has grown at tremendous rate for the past 6 to 7 years as the influx of new Islamic banks have created the much required depth in the industry. There is a need to revisit the study as more financial institutions such as development financial institutions also provide Islamic banking products albeit minimal in terms of ranges of products.

Given the nature of the DFIs, the size of financing albeit small in number but might be significant in terms of value. These Islamic finance portfolios are not included in the study as the requirement of RWCAR reporting only applies to full-fledged Islamic Financial Institutions (IFIs). The inclusion of these unaccounted portfolios could also provide further insights into the relationships with RWCAR of Islamic Banks in Malaysia.

This is the platform that this research shall leave and it would be a great honour if someone were to carry it further. Maybe the answer is already there in front of us; maybe the world does not wish to see. Maybe we have been barking at the wrong tree all along.

Bibliography

Abdelaziz Chazi and Lateef A.M. Syed, (2010), "Risk exposure during the global financial crisis: the case of Islàmic banks", *International Journal of Islamic and Middle Eastern Finance and Management*, Vol. 3, No. 4, pp. 321-333

Abul Hassan, (2009), "Risk management practices of Islamic banks of Brunei Darussalam", *The Journal of Risk Finance*, Vol. 10, No. 1, pp. 23-37

Adel Ahmed, (2010), "Global financial crisis: an Islamic finance perspective", *International Journal of Islamic and Middle Eastern Finance and Management*, Vol. 3, No. 4, pp. 306-320

Al-Awan, Malik Muhammad Mahmud, 2006, "Globalization of Islamic funds," *Islamic Banking and Finance, issue,* Vol. 11, pp. 14-15

Alessandro Carretta, Vincenzo Farina, Paola Schwiser, (2010), "Assessing effectiveness and compliance of banking boards", *Journal of Financial Regulation and Compliance*, Vol.18, No.4, pp. 356-369

Archer, S. and Abdel Karim, R.A (2002), "Introduction to Islamic finance", in Archer, S. and Abdel Karim, R.A. (Eds), Islamic Finance: Innovation and Growth, Euromoney Books, London, pp. 9-26

Arzu, T., Nur, O.G., Gokhan, G. (2005), "Asset and liability management in financial crisis", *The Journal of Risk Finance*, Vol. 6, No. 2, pp.135-49

Basel Committtee on Banking Supervision, Bank of International Settlements (2009), History of the Basel Committee and its Membership (August 2009)

Cadbury Committee (1992), Report of the Committee on the Financial Aspects of Corporate Governance, Gee & Co., London

Chau, G.K. and Gray, S.J. (200), "Ownership structure and corporate voluntary disclosure in Hong Kong and Singapore", *The International Journal of Accounting*, Vol.37 No.2, pp 247-64

Christos Alexakis, Alexandros Tsikouras, (2009), "Islamic finance: regulatory framework—challenges lying ahead", *International Journal of Islamic and Middle Eastern Finance and Management*, Vol.2, No. 2 pp. 90-104

Claessens, S. Djankov, S. Fan, J.P.H and Lang, L.H.P (1999), "Corporate diversification in East Asia: the role of ultimate ownership and group affiliation", working paper No. 2089, World Bank, Washington, DC.

Estrella, A., Park, S. and Peristani, S. (2000), "Capital ratios as predictors of bank failures", *FBRNY Economic Policy Review*, Vol. 6, No. 23, pp. 33-52

Fauziah Hanim Tafri, Rashidah Abdul Rahman, Normah Omar, (2011), "Empirical evidence on the risk management tools practised in Islamic and conventional banks", *Qualitative Research in Financial Markets*, Vol. 3 No. 2 pp. 86-104

Gerhard Kling and Utz Weitzel, (2011), "The internationalization of Chinese companies: Firm characteristics, industry effects and corporate governance", *Research in International Business and Finance*, Vol.25, pp 357-372

Hameeda Abu Hussain, Jasim Al-Ajmi, (2012), "Risk management practices of conventional and Islamic banks in Bahrain", *The Journal of Risk Finance*, Vol. 13, No. 3, pp. 215-239

Hanudin Amin, Abdul Rahim Abdul Rahman, Stephen Laison Sondoh Jr, Ang Magdalene Chooi Hwa, (2011), "Determinants of customers' intention to use Islamic personal financing—The case of Malaysian Islamic bank", *Journal of Islamic Accounting and Business Research*, Vol.2, No. 1, 2011, pp. 22-42

Helder Ferreira de Mendoca, Delio Jose Cordeiro Galvao, Renato Falci Villela Loures, (2012), "Financial regulation and transparency of information: evidence from banking industry", *Journal of Economic Studies*, Vol.39, No. 4 pp. 380-397

Iman Khanchel, (2007), "Corporate governance: measurement and determinant analysis", *Managerial Auditing Journal*, Vol.22 No. 8, pp 740-760

Imran Tahir, Mark Brimble, (2011), "Islamic investment behaviour", *International Journal of Islamic and Middle Eastern Finance and Management*, Vol. 4, No.2, 2011, pp. 116-130

International Centre for Education in Islamic Finance, (2006), Applied Shariah in Financial Transactions, Chartered Islamic Finance Professional—Part 1 Study Material. ISBN No: 983-3729-03-7

International Centre for Education in Islamic Finance, (2006), Islamic Economics and Finance: Theory and Ethics, Chartered

Islamic Finance Professional—Part 1 Study Material. ISBN No: 983-3729-00-2

Islamic Banking and Takaful Department, (2010), Capital Adequacy Framework for Islamic Banks (CAFIB), Guidelines No: BNM/RH/GL002-14, Bank Negara Malaysia

Islamic Banking and Takaful Department, (2012), Capital Adequacy Framework for Islamic Banks (CAFIB)—Internal Capital Adequacy Assessment Process (Pillar 2), Guidelines No: BNM/RH/GL002-22, Bank Negara Malaysia

Islamic Banking and Takaful Department, (2012), Capital Adequacy Framework for Islamic Banks (CAFIB) (Risk Weighted Assets), Guidelines No: BNM/RH/GL007-21, Bank Negara Malaysia

Islamic Banking and Takaful Department, Guidelines on Corporate Governance for Licensed Islamic Bank", GP1-i, Guidelines No: BNM/RH/GL002-1, Bank Negara Malaysia

Islamic Financial Services Board (IFSB), (2005), Capital Adequacy Standard for Institutions (Other than Insurance Institutions) Offering Only Islamic Financial Services (CAS), IFSB.

Ivan E. Brick, N.K. Chidambran, (2010), "Board meetings, committte structure, and firm value, Journal of Corporate Finance, Vol.16, pp. 533-553

Jaana Lappalainen, Mervi Niskanen, (2012), "Financial Performance of SMEs—Impact of Ownership Strudture and Board Composition", *Management Research Review*, Vol. 35, No. 11 (Date online 28/8/2012)

Jensen, M.C. and Meckling, W. (1976), "Theory of the firm: managerial behaviour, agency costs, and ownership structure", *Journal of Financial Economics*, Vol.3, pp. 305-60

Kosmas Kosmidis, Konstantinos Terzidis, "Manipulating an IRB model: considerations about the Basel II framework", *EuroMed Journal of Business*, Vol. 6, No. 2 pp. 174-191

KPMG International (2006), KPMG Islamic Finance Credentials, KPMG International, Amstelveen.

La Porta, R., Lopz-De-Silanes, F., Shleifer, A. and Vishy, R. (2000), "Investor protection and corporate governance", *Journal of Financial Economics*, Vol.58, Nos 1/2, pp 3-27

M. Mansoor Khan, M. Ishaq Bhatti, (2008), "Development in Islamic banking: a financial risk—allocation approach", *The Journal of Risk Finance*, Vol. 9, No. 1, pp. 40-51

Mark. A. Bliss, Balachandran Muniandy, Abdul Majid (2007), "CEO duality, audit committee effectiveness and audit risks: A study of the Malaysian market," *Managerial Auditing Journal*, Vol.22 No. 7, pp. 716-728

Mazlina Mustapha, Ayoib Che Ahmad, (2011), "Agency theory and managerial ownership: evidence from Malaysia", *Managerial Auditing Journal*, Vol. 26, No. 5 pp.419-436

Michael Mainelli, (2011), "Money in a time of choleric: Basel blows the bubbles", *The Journal of Risk Finance*, Vol. 12 No. 4, pp. 348-350

Mohd Hassan Che Haat, Rashidah Abdul Rahman, Sakthi Mahenthiran (2008), "Corporate governance, transparency and performance of Malaysian companies", *Managerial Auditing Journal*, Vol. 23, No. 8 pp. 744-778

Nadeem Ahmed Sheikh, Zongjun Wang, (2012), "Effects of corporate governance on capital structure: empirical evidence from Pakistan", Corporate Governance, Vol. 12, No. 5 (Date online 12/8/2012)

Nava Subramaniam, Lisa McManus, Jiani Zhang, (2009), "Corporate governance, firm characteristics and risk management committee formation in Australian companies", *Managerial Auditing Journal*, Vol. 24, No. 4, pp 316-339

Norhani Aripin, Greg Tower, Grantley Taylor,(2011), "Insights on the diversity of financial ratios communication", *Asian Review of Accounting*, Vol.19, NO. 1 pp.68-85

Patelli, L. and Prencipe, A. (2007), "The relationship between voluntary disclosure and independent directors in the presence of a dominant shareholder", *European Accounting Review*, Vol. 16, No. 1, pp. 5-33

Saiful Azhar Rosly, Mohammad Ashadi Mohd Zaini, 2008, "Risk-return analysis of Islamic banks' investment deposits and shareholders' fund", *Managerial Finance*, Vol. 34, No. 10, 2008, pp. 695-707

Sanjay Peters, Mariah Miller, Sophia Kusyk, (2011), "How relevant is corporate governance and corporate social responsibility in emerging markets?", *Corporate Governance*, Vol.11, No. 4 pp. 429-445

Securities Commission Malaysia (2012), Malaysian Code on Corporate Governance 2012.

Seung-Rok Park, Ky-hyang Yuhn, (2012), "Has the Korean chaebol model succeeded?", *Journal of Economic Studies*, Vol. 39, No. 2, pp. 260-274

Simon Archer, Rifaat Ahmed Abdel Karim, Venkataraman Sundararajan, (2010), "Supervisory, regulatory and capital adequacy implications of profit—sharing investment accounts in Islamic finance", *Journal of Islamic Accounting and Business Research*, Vol. 1, No. 1 pp.10-31

Siti Sakinah Azizan, Rashid Ameer, (2012), "Shareholder activism in family—controlled firms in Malaysia", *Managerial Auditing Journal*, Vol. 27, No. 8, pp. 774-794

Soo Wook Kim, (2011), "The quality impact of governance change on board decision making", *Asian Journal on Quality*, Vol.12 No. 1, pp 113-123.

Yermack, D. (1996), "Higher market valuation of companies with a small board of directors", *Journal of Financial Economics*, Vol. 40, pp. 185-211

Zaini Embong, Norman Mohd-Salleh, Mohamat Sabri Hassan, (2012), "Firm size, disclosure and cost of equity capital", *Asian Review of Accounting*, Vol. 20 No. 2 pp. 119-139

Zulkifli Hassan, (2011), "A survery on Shari'ah governance practices in Malaysia, GCC countries and the UK: Critical appraisal", *International Journal of Islamic and Middle Eastern Finance and Management*, Vol.4, No. 1 pp.30-51

Appendix 1

Research Sampling and Development of Constructs

To date, there are 16 of Islamic Banks operating in Malaysia (source: Bank Negara Malaysia) as follows:

i)   Affin Islamic Bank Berhad
ii)   Al Rajhi Banking & Investment Corporation (M) Berhad
iii)   Alliance Islamic Bank Berhad
iv)   AmIslamic Bank Berhad
v)   Asian Finance Bank Berhad
vi)   Bank Islam Malaysia Berhad
vii)   Bank Muamalat Malaysia Berhad
viii)   CIMB Islamic Bank Berhad
ix)   EONCAP Islamic Bank Berhad*
x)   Hong Leong Islamic Bank Berhad
xi)   HSBC Amanah Malaysia Berhad
xii)   Kuwait Finance House (M) Berhad
xiii)   Maybank Islamic Berhad
xiv)   OCBC Al-Amin Bank Berhad
xv)   Public Islamic Bank Berhad
xvi)   RHB Islamic Bank Berhad
xvii)   Standard Chartered Saadiq Berhad

Given that there is only 16 full fledge Islamic banks in Malaysia, the entire population is used for this study. The secondary information for this study shall be obtained from the audited financial statements and the annual reports of all Islamic banks in Malaysia and shall be keyed into SPSS. In addition, to fully optimise the sample size and to identify and study trends, the data shall be collected for the past 3 years since 2009. This is also pertinent since these data are post 2008 global financial crisis which is in line with the studies by Chazi & Syed (2010) that Islamic banks globally were able to weather the adverse effects from the financial crisis in 2008 due to the risk aversion mechanisms inherent in basic Islamic finance principles.

For the information that are unable to be sourced from the audited report of a particular Islamic Banks such as effective foreign ownership or number of Board meetings, these information are approximated by using the data available on the annual report of the holding company. For example, since Public Islamic Bank Berhad is a wholly owned subsidiary of Public Bank Berhad, therefore, the data for effective foreign shareholding is derived using the effective percentage of foreign shareholding disclosed in Public Bank Berhad's annual report for the same period.

Appendix 2

Bank Negara Malaysia's Adaption of Basel I Risk Weighting

Type of Bank Assets (Basel I)	Basel I Risk Weighting	Adapted by Bank Negara Malaysia (BNM)	BNM Weighting
Cash, central bank and government debt or any OECD	0%	• Cash or claims collateralised by cash; • Claims on (including reverse repos with BNM), guaranteed by, or collateralised by securities issued by the Federal Government of Malaysia and the Central Bank of Malaysia (BNM); • Claims on and guaranteed by the Organisation for Economic Cooperation and Development (OECD) central governments and central banks; • Claims collateralised by securities (including repos and reverse repos of securities) issued by the OECD central governments; • Claims on non-OECD central governments and central banks denominated in the national currency (of the debtor) and funded by liabilities in the same currency; • Ringgit denominated bonds issued by Multilateral Development Banks (MDB) and Multilateral Financial Institutions (MFIs); • Holdings of ABF Malaysia Bond Index Fund;	0%

Type of Bank Assets (Basel I)	Basel I Risk Weighting	Adapted by Bank Negara Malaysia (BNM)	BNM Weighting
		• Exposure to ringgit denominated bonds issued by non-resident quasi-sovereign agencies that fulfil the following requirements: i) Issue has an explicit guarantee from or is wholly/majority owned by the sovereign (federal government) or central bank (where the issuer is incorporated); ii) The issuer is specifically accorded a 0% risk weight by the national supervisor (where the issuer is incorporated); and iii) The issuer's sovereign or central bank is rated at least A-; • Loans guaranteed by Credit Guarantee Corporation (CGC) under the SME Assistance Guarantee Scheme.	
Public sector debt	0%, 10%, 20% or 50% (optional)	• Holdings of Cagamas debt securities issued before 4 Sept 2004 • Other claims on Cagamas Berhad (Cagamas)	10%

84

Type of Bank Assets (Basel I)	Basel I Risk Weighting	Adapted by Bank Negara Malaysia (BNM)	BNM Weighting
Development Bank debt, OECD bank debt, OECD securities firm debt, non-OECD bank debt (under one year maturity) and non-OECD public sector debt, cash in collection	20%	• Claims, guarantees or securities issued by licensed banks in Malaysia (including foreign banks operating in Malaysia); • Claims and guarantees issued by banks incorporated in OECD member countries; • Claims, guarantees or securities issued by domestic development financial institutions; • Claims, guarantees or securities issued by other MDBs (that are not eligible for 0% weighting above); • Claims and guarantees by banks outside the OECD (with maturity of less than 1 year); • Claims and guarantees by OECD public sector companies (excluding central government) • Equity investments in CGC • CGC guaranteed portions of all new Principal Guarantee Scheme Loans • Cagamas HKC Berhad guaranteed portions of loans secured by mortgages on residential property	

Type of Bank Assets (Basel I)	Basel I Risk Weighting	Adapted by Bank Negara Malaysia (BNM)	BNM Weighting
		• Housing loans, hire purchase and leasing debts sold to Cagamas; • Tranche 1 to 4 of Real Estate Mortgage Backed Securities (RMBS) issued by Cagamas; • Holdings of Cagamas securities after 4 Sept 2004; • Islamic CP/MTN programme issued by Rantau Abang Capital Berhad (wholly owned by Khazanah Nasional Bhd)	
n/a	n/a	• Performing residential property loans with Loan to Value (LTV) ratio of less than 80%.	35%
Residential mortgages	50%	• Other performing residential property loans	50%

Type of Bank Assets (Basel I)	Basel I Risk Weighting	Adapted by Bank Negara Malaysia (BNM)	BNM Weighting
Private sector debt, non-OECD bank debt (maturing over a year), real estate, plant and equipment, capital instruments issued at other banks.	100%	• Claims on banks incorporated outside OECD with maturity of more than 1 year; • Capital instruments rated BB - and above issued by foreign incorporated banks; • Claims on non-OECD central governments not denominated and funded in the national currency; • Claims on private companies owned by Non-Financial Public Enterprises; • Investments in shares (not deducted from the capital base); • Loans and advances to corporate and corporate debt securities rated BB- and above; • Private sector loans collateralised by residential property; • • Unsecured portion of housing loan/overdraft facility • Non Performing Loan secured by first charge; • Housing loans, hire purchase and leasing loans purchased from non banks and sold to Cagamas under back to back arrangement; • Claims from universal brokers;	100%

Type of Bank Assets (Basel I)	Basel I Risk Weighting	Adapted by Bank Negara Malaysia (BNM)	BNM Weighting
		• Capital instruments of other licensed banks which are transferred from trading account to banking account; • All other assets; and • Mudharabah deposits or profit-sharing investment account deposits placed by parent banks in Islamic subsidiaries	
N/A		• Claims on corporate rated below BB-; • Capital instruments of ratings below BB- issued by foreign incorporated banks.	150%